The Life of The Last Prophet

The Life of The Last Prophet

By

YUSUF ISLAM

DARUSSALAM
Publishers & Distributors
Riyadh, Saudi Arabia

This edition first published in 1996
by Mountain of Light
PO Box 7404 London N7 8JQ UK

British Libary Cataloguing in Publication Data
A catalogue record of this book is available
from The British Library
Library of Congress Catalog Card Number
96-76107

ISBN 1900675 00 5

Printing of this edition supervised by
Abdul Malik Mujahid

DARUSSALAM
Publishers & Distributors
Riyadh, Saudi Arabia
Tel:00-966-1-4033962.4043432

CONTENTS

Introduction	vii
The Call to Prayer	xi
Early Life	1
Prophethood	7
Migration	21
Conquest of Makkah	33
Sayings of the Prophet ص	39
Notes	43
Chronology	49
Du'ā	51

Introduction

'WE HAVE SENT YOU (O MUHAMMAD)
ONLY AS A MERCY FOR ALL THE WORLDS.'

QUR'AN: THE PROPHETS (21):107

THE BIRTH of the Prophet of Islam, peace and blessings be upon him, and the dawn of his prophethood was not the birth of a Prophet alone, nor was it the rise of a new nation, nor yet the beginning of a new era. It was the genesis of a new world which was destined to last till the end of time when all shall be returned to their Lord and Master. The influence of Muhammad's prophethood is visible in everything that the world now contains, the beliefs and patterns of thought, culture and civilization, morals and modes of living, knowledge and learning. In short, all spheres of human endeavour.[1]

Strange indeed, therefore, that so many people on the face of the earth today have little or no knowledge of the life and mission of this last great Prophet of God and his historical impact on the world we live in. It is for this reason that it was decided in all humility to try and compile a brief account of the major highlights of his biography for the general public.

Endless are the words which have been spoken to describe his noble life and personality, but the aim of this presentation is to keep the story as authentic and simple as possible. It is intended as an introduction for those perhaps approaching the subject of the Prophet for the first time. I believe no one can fail to be moved or inspired by the magnificence of his radiant character: even Muhammad's greatest enemies had to admit that no fault could be found in his behaviour or integrity. In addition, those Western scholars and historical figures who over the centuries were brave enough to gaze with an honest heart at the miracle of Muhammad's life and achievements, have testified to this. Some of their observations are remarkable. For example, George Bernard Shaw said:

> *"I believe that if a man like him were to assume the dictatorship of the modern world, he would succeed in solving the problems in a way that would bring the much needed peace and happiness. Europe is beginning to be enamoured of the creed of Muhammad. In the next century it may go further in recognizing the utility of that creed in solving its problems."* [2]

Lamartine in his lengthy tribute to the Prophet wrote:

> *"If greatness of purpose, smallness of means and astounding results are the three criteria of human genius, who could claim to compare any great man in modern history with Muhammad?"* [3]

Perhaps most telling of all, Gandhi wrote the following about the Prophet of Islam:

> *"I become more than ever convinced that it was not the sword that won a place for Islam in those days. It was the rigid simplicity, the utter self-effacement of the Prophet, the scrupulous regard for pledges, his intense devotion to his friends and followers and his intrepidity, his fearlessness, his absolute trust in God and in his own mission. These and not the sword carried everything before them and surmounted every obstacle."* [4]

This very concise account of 'The Life of the Last Prophet' can in no way take the place of those precious volumes – the product of many years of devoted research – which a great constellation of scholars and historians, such as Ibn Ishaq and Ibn Hisham, have contributed to the understanding and study of the subject; nor does it attempt to. My only hope is simply that it will be able to kindle a spark of light and understanding and inspire the seeker of truth to proceed further along the Way of Guidance that leads to God and earns His good pleasure and eternal mercy.

I seek forgiveness from Allah the Most High for any mistake or error made in the execution of this task, beseeching Him for His pardon; praying for the guidance of those who may hear it and choose, by the will of God, to follow the noble Messenger.

All praise is due to Allah, Lord of the worlds and may He send His choicest salutations and peace on the Seal of the Prophets, Muhammad, and upon his Family and Companions together, *Amin*.

YUSUF ISLAM 1416H/1995CE

REFERENCES:

1. Abul Hasan Ali Nadwi, *Islamic Concept of Prophethood.*
2. George Bernard Shaw, *A Collection of Writing of Some of the Eminent Scholars*, 1935.
3. Lamartine, *Histoire de la Turquie*, 1855.
4. Gandhi, *Young India*, 1922.

ACKNOWLEDGEMENTS:

Khurram Murad; Dr. Muhammad Isa Waley; Dr. Syed Mutawalli Darsh; Sara Sharif; Dr. Mirza Azam Baig; Ghulam Sarwar; Dr. Farouk S. Shaheen; Shaykh Suhaib Hasan; Muhammad Morgan; Tayyeb Shah; Rashid Ayyub.

PHOTOCREDITS:

Peter Sanders; Tony Stone Images.

DESIGN:

Abd al-Lateef Whiteman and Yusuf Islam

The Call to Prayer

Allāhu akbar! Allāhu akbar! Allāhu akbar! Allāhu akbar! Ashhadu an lā ilāha illa Allāh. Ashhadu an lā ilāha illa Allāh. Ashhadu anna Muḥammadan Rasūlu Allāh. Ashhadu anna Muḥammadan Rasūlu Allāh. Ḥayya 'ala al-ṣalāh. Ḥayya 'ala al-ṣalāh. Ḥayya 'ala al-falāḥ. Ḥayya 'ala al-falāḥ. Allāhu akbar! Allāhu akbar! Lā ilāha illa Allāh. Allah is Most Great! Allah is Most Great! Allah is Most Great! Allah is Most Great! I bear witness that there is no god but Allah. I bear witness that there is no god but Allah. I bear witness that Muhammad is the messenger of Allah. I bear witness that Muhammad is the messenger of Allah. Come to prayer. Come to prayer. Come to success. Come to success. Allah is Most Great! Allah is Most Great! There is no god but Allah.[1]

Early Life

MUHAMMAD, *ṣalla Allāhu 'alayhi wa sallam*,[2] peace and blessings of Allah be upon him, was a mercy to the universe. His life ever shines as a symbol of light and guidance for all time and for all people. He was the last Messenger of God to humanity, the Seal of the Prophets. To the oneness of God he called – *Lā ilāha illa Allāh, Muḥammadun Rasūlu Allāh*: there is no god but Allah, Muhammad is the Messenger of Allah. This is the life and message of Islam.

THE LONE ORPHAN

Muhammad, *ṣalla Allāhu 'alayhi wa sallam*, the Last Prophet, was born in the harsh desert land of Arabia almost 600 years after Jesus, peace be upon him, in the city of Makkah, located in a deep valley surrounded by a curtain of brown and black jagged mountains.

Muhammad, *ṣalla Allāhu 'alayhi wa sallam*, was an orphan. His father had died before he was born. So he was raised and weaned in the desert according to Arab custom. By the tender age of six, his mother Aminah also died and he was left all alone to be brought up by his grandfather 'Abd al-Muttalib and later under the care of his paternal uncle Abu Talib.

Makkah was an important and famous city, primarily because within it stood the Holy Ka'bah, the First House ever set up for mankind to glorify the one true God, constructed some three thousand years earlier[3] by the Prophet Abraham with the help of his first son Ishmael, peace be upon them. It was here in this deserted and barren valley that Abraham, according to Divine Will, had settled his wife Hajar along with their child Ishmael. So it was that with the passage of time Makkah gradually became a city of pilgrimage and a flourishing centre of culture and trade, through which passed the great trade caravans between Syria in the north and Yemen in the south. Muhammad, *ṣalla Allāhu 'alayhi wa sallam,* was a direct descendant of Abraham through Ishmael, belonging to the noble and renowned family of Bani Hashim.

As a shepherd boy, Muhammad, *ṣalla Allāhu 'alayhi wa sallam,* used to tend the sheep and goats around the hills of Makkah, under the bright burning sun: a familiar training, it seems, for those destined to fulfil the role of prophethood.

THE TRUSTWORTHY

As a young man, Muhammad became known to everybody as *al-Amin,* 'the Trustworthy', because of his honesty and noble character. His uncle loved him dearly and would take him on trading journeys to Syria. This gave Muhammad, *ṣalla Allāhu 'alayhi wa sallam,* the opportunity to learn how to earn his living as a trader. He managed business well. Although he was relatively poor, Muhammad's truthfulness and generous nature made him trusted and loved by everyone who knew him.

There lived in Makkah one of the most honourable of ladies: her name was Khadijah. Muhammad, *ṣalla Allāhu 'alayhi wa sallam,* had worked for her and at the age of twenty-five he received from her an indirect proposal of marriage. Although she was his senior and twice widowed, Muhammad, *ṣalla Allāhu 'alayhi wa sallam,* accepted her offer. They were married and lived a happy life. She bore him two sons and four daughters.[4] Sadly, the two sons died in infancy; nevertheless, it was an ideal marriage and they lived together a blissfully perfect family life.

THE BLACK STONE

Muhammad's company and wise counsel were greatly sought after. It is said that once, when the sacred Ka'bah was being rebuilt after a serious flood had damaged its walls, a disagreement arose amongst the four main tribes of the Quraysh as to which tribe should have the honour of replacing the sacred Black Stone. A skirmish was about to begin, when one of the elders suggested a solution: "Make the first to enter the gate your judge," he said. They all looked, and to their great joy, Muhammad entered. "It is *al-Amin*, the Trustworthy," they cried. Muhammad, *ṣalla Allāhu 'alayhi wa sallam,* saw what was happening and he asked for a piece of cloth to be brought. He laid the Black Stone upon the cloth and told the members of each of the four tribes to hold the corners of the cloth and raise the Stone as he, himself, eased it into its position. So, he ended the quarrel and with it the threat of war.[5]

The Arabs of his time had many great qualities. They were brave, generous, loyal and yet they were often involved in petty feuds, fighting endless battles amongst themselves, ready to shed blood on the flimsiest pretext. They had little respect for the weak, the orphans or widows and frequently indulged in heavy drinking and frivolity. Because of the important status given to sons, many fathers practised the evil custom of burying their unwanted daughters at birth. But, at the root of all evils lay polytheism.

POLYTHEISTS AND IDOLS

Polytheism, the cult of worshipping idols, was practised by almost everyone. The everlasting religion and legacy of Abraham – the worship of one true God alone – had been buried and forgotten with time. Over the years, some 360 idols and statues of false gods had been installed in and around the Holy Ka'bah, worshipped as lords and intercessors.[6] Even the followers of Moses and Jesus had diverged from the universality and teachings of the pure monotheistic faith of Abraham and had divided themselves into many separate sects and tribes.

But Muhammad, *ṣalla Allāhu 'alayhi wa sallam,* was an exceptional figure. He did not take part in any of this. It became his habit in later years to retreat to an isolated cave in the nearby mountain called Hira, not far from Makkah, to bare his heart and pray in search of Truth. With no sound but the stirring wind, he would contemplate, in his solitude, the signs of the universe.

Prophethood

IT WAS HERE, one night during the month of Ramadan, at the age of 40, that the Almighty called Muhammad, *ṣalla Allāhu 'alayhi wa sallam,* to His service. This Night, known as *Laylat al-Qadr,* 'The Night of Power', the Spirit of Truth was to descend with God's Decree and Light for humanity: the Qur'an. A new chapter for the world was about to unfold.

THE CAVE

The white waning moon was shining brightly when suddenly, he perceived a presence. Out of the stillness of the night, a voice was heard. "Read!" Muhammad was shaken. "I cannot read," he replied. The earth seemed to tremble as the voice repeated the command, pressing him on, "Read!" "I cannot read." He felt himself frozen with fear, unable to move. "Read!" The awesome voice commanded again. "What shall I read?"[7] Then suddenly he was released; at that moment, all time and space were still. Peace – as mankind stood at the threshold of a new dawn.

'IQRA' bismi Rabbika al-ladhī khalaq • Khalaqa al-insāna min 'alaq • 'Iqra' wa Rabbuka al-Akram • Al-ladhī 'allama bi-al-qalam • 'Allama al-insāna mā lam ya'lam • READ! IN THE NAME OF YOUR LORD WHO CREATES • CREATES MAN FROM A CLOT OF BLOOD • READ! AND YOUR LORD IS MOST GENEROUS • WHO TEACHES BY THE PEN • TEACHES MAN THAT WHICH HE KNEW NOT •[8]

These were the first five jewelled verses of the Glorious Qur'an. The voice was that of Angel Gabriel, the Spirit of Faith and Truth, who had been sent to the last of God's Prophets. The mission had just begun for Muhammad, *ṣalla Allāhu 'alayhi wa sallam*, the Messenger of Allah – a mercy to the worlds.

The Prophet Muhammad, *ṣalla Allāhu 'alayhi wa sallam*, had just received the first words from his Lord on Mount Hira. He rushed down from the mountain, his face shining with beads of sweat, heart beating fiercely. The verses of the Qur'an were still echoing in his soul. What kind of visitation was this, what kind of words? He ran to Khadijah, "Cover me! Cover me!" She gently comforted him as he explained what had just happened. "I fear that something may befall me," he said. "Never! By Allah," said his wife faithfully.

"Allah would never disgrace you. You keep good relations with all your relatives, you help the poor and the needy, you serve your guests generously and assist the deserving unfortunate ones."[9]

Some time later Khadijah took him to her cousin, a learned scribe named Waraqah, who knew the Torah and the Gospel well. After describing to him what had happened that night, the old man, without hesitation, affirmed that indeed this must have been a meeting with Archangel Gabriel, whom Allah had sent to Moses. "I wish I were young and could live up to the time when your people turn you out," the old wise man said.[10] He knew that the Prophet foretold in the earlier Scriptures had arrived. So began the call of the Last Prophet, *ṣalla Allāhu 'alayhi wa sallam*, which was to influence the world forevermore and herald a new age in the history of human consciousness and progress; the birth of Islam.

The first to believe in the Prophet, *ṣalla Allāhu 'alayhi wa sallam*, was his wife Khadijah, followed shortly after by his young beloved cousin 'Ali, son of Abu Talib, who lived with them. Most were violently opposed but some willingly opened their hearts and accepted the call, like Muhammad's closest friend and companion, Abu Bakr and his servant Zayd and others.

After a while, as the revelations of the Qur'an continued, the Prophet, *ṣalla Allāhu 'alayhi wa sallam*, was commanded to publicly deliver the message of Islam and recite the verses which had been sent to him.

BISMI Allāhi al-Raḥmāni al-Raḥīm • Al-Ḥamdu lillāhi Rabbi al-'ālamīn • Al-Raḥmāni al-Raḥīm • Māliki yawmi al-dīn • Iyyāka na'budu wa iyyāka nasta'īn • Ihdina al-Ṣirāṭ al-mustaqīm • Ṣirāṭa al-ladhīna an'amta 'alayhim ghayri al-maghḍūbi 'alayhim wa la al-ḍāllīn •

IN THE NAME OF ALLAH, THE BENEFICENT, THE MERCIFUL • PRAISE BE TO ALLAH, LORD OF THE WORLDS • THE BENEFICENT, THE MERCIFUL • MASTER OF THE DAY OF JUDGEMENT • YOU ALONE WE WORSHIP AND YOU ALONE WE ASK FOR HELP • SHOW US THE STRAIGHT PATH • THE PATH OF THOSE WHOM YOU HAVE FAVOURED, NOT THOSE WHO EARN YOUR ANGER, NOR THOSE WHO GO ASTRAY • [11]

One day the Prophet, *ṣalla Allāhu 'alayhi wa sallam*, climbed to the top of Safa, a small hillock close to the sacred Ka'bah, and called out to his kinsmen, the people of Quraysh. As they gathered around him, they asked him what was the matter. Muhammad, *ṣalla Allāhu 'alayhi wa sallam*, answered. "Tell me (o men of Makkah), if I were to inform you that I see an army on the other side of this hill, would you believe me?" "Indeed!" they all answered, "for we trust you and we know you never tell a lie." "Then," Muhammad said, "know that I am a warner and that I warn you of a severe punishment…God has commanded me to warn you, my nearest kin, that I can guarantee you no good on earth or in the heavens." The crowd, on hearing this, became dumbstruck. As they stood silent and still under the heat of the sun, Abu Lahab[12], the Prophet's uncle, finally burst out, "May you perish!" They all turned their backs and dispersed leaving Muhammad, *ṣalla Allāhu 'alayhi wa sallam,* standing alone.

REJECTION

The people of Makkah listened to these new words calling them to bow to Allah and to enter the religion of loving submission – Islam. But soon they became sharply divided. Many began to reject the glaring truth. After years of knowing Muhammad, *ṣalla Allāhu 'alayhi wa sallam,* as the most kind and pious among them, they started insulting him and ridiculing him and even calling him insane. Yet with all this abuse hurled upon him, he would never speak a bad word in return. He used to say, "He who believes in Allah and the Last Day, should be good to his guest. He who believes in Allah and the Last Day, should honour his neighbour. And he who believes in Allah and the Last Day, should say what is good or be silent." [13]

Nothing would deter him. He continued patiently inviting his townsfolk to what was the first basic pillar of Islam: to bear witness that there was no god worthy of worship but Allah, and that he, Muhammad, was the Messenger of Allah.

The more he called them to submit to the one and only God, the more enraged the tribal chiefs became. "What!" they said, "has he made all our gods into one God? This is a strange thing indeed." [14] What was even more surprising to them was that these miraculous new words – the passages of the Qur'an – were coming to a man who they knew was unlettered. Never had Muhammad, *ṣalla Allāhu 'alayhi wa sallam,* learned to read or write, a skill that only a few could claim amongst the Arabs at that time. So how then were these words, so matchless in their beauty and articulation, coming to him?

QUL Huwa Allāhu Aḥad • Allāhu al-Ṣamad • Lam yalid wa lam yūlad • Wa lam yakun lahū kufuwan aḥad •

SAY: HE IS ALLAH, THE ONE • ALLAH, THE ETERNAL, ABSOLUTE • HE BEGETS NOT, NOR WAS HE BEGOTTEN • AND THERE IS NONE COMPARABLE TO HIM • [15]

The chiefs of the Quraysh, the most influential tribe in Makkah, became more and more enraged.

However, at one of their council meetings, they decided to ask the Prophet's uncle and guardian, Abu Talib, to mediate, to try and stop him from calling people away from their customs and the religion of their forefathers.

Muhammad, *ṣalla Allāhu 'alayhi wa sallam*, when he heard this, was emotionally moved, because of the love and affection he felt for his dear uncle, but his answer was calm and clear: "By Allah! If they placed the sun in my right hand and moon in my left, I would never abandon this course until Allah makes it victorious, or I die therein." [16]

Slowly, one by one, the number of Muslims grew, under the guidance of the beloved Prophet, *ṣalla Allāhu 'alayhi wa sallam*. This first noble group of believers followed the way of righteousness and submission. Their love for the Truth shone out, illuminating the dull paganistic society of that time. The pursuit of worldly gain – the main objective of earthly life and ambitions – was shunned in favour of the pursuit of eternal Light and wisdom. "Whoever follows a path to seek knowledge therein," the Prophet, *ṣalla Allāhu 'alayhi wa sallam*, said, "Allah will make easy for him the path to Paradise." [17]

Yet Muslims were made the object of persecution from the very beginning. Those who were poor, of little means and had no position, suffered the most.

They were mocked and laughed at, but when ridicule failed, the disbelievers resorted to physical attacks and torment. Stones and dirt were hurled at them. Some hundred Muslims were permitted to leave Makkah, abandoning their homes, and seeking refuge in neighbouring Abyssinia, a Christian land. [18]

For those who stayed behind, the persecution increased. Bilal, a black Abyssinian slave, who had accepted Islam, was laid outstretched on the burning sand at the behest of his brutal master, whilst large heavy rocks were placed on his chest. "Where is your God now?" the disbelievers taunted him, but no amount of torture could shake his faith. The believers would never give up Islam.

BOYCOTT

So a new tactic was adopted by the chiefs of Makkah. The Prophet, *ṣalla Allāhu 'alayhi wa sallam*, and his followers were evicted and forced to live in a confined section of town. No provisions were allowed to get through to them and they had to suffer long torturous periods without food or water, not eating for days or even weeks on end. This boycott began in the seventh year after the commencement of the Qur'anic revelation and lasted for three long years, but by the Grace of Allah, some kind hearts amongst the persecutors could not tolerate the victimization any longer. Their will gradually softened and the ban was finally lifted.

Again, the people were able to observe and listen to

the Prophet, *ṣalla Allāhu 'alayhi wa sallam*. He was the most handsome of men, of medium height, black hair and beard. His teeth shone gleaming white when he smiled. But it was his character and perfect behaviour which made the greatest impression. His words were always full of guidance and wisdom. The customs and traditions of the tribal society in Arabia were shaken and revised by the extraordinary spirit of his teachings. He said, "Support your brother, whether he is doing wrong or he has been wronged." A man enquired, "O Messenger of Allah! I can help him if he has been wronged, but how can I support him if he is doing wrong?" He said, "Prevent him from doing wrong: that is how you support him."[19]

Muhammad's kindness and merciful nature was also unparalleled. Often, when he passed by a group of children, he would pass his hand affectionately over their heads and sometimes would even join in innocent games. He said, "There are for Allah one hundred mercies, of which only one was sent down among the jinn, mankind, beasts, birds and insects. Through it they incline towards each other, through it they show mercy to one another and through it they show affection towards their younger ones. And Allah has reserved for Himself ninety-nine mercies with which He will show mercy to His servants on the Day of Resurrection."[20]

He gave special place and honour to women. In one stroke Islam raised them to a position unimaginable in the society at that time, guaranteeing them rights and liberties not equalled anywhere. Paradise lies at the feet of the mother, he said.[21] But the majority still persisted in their ways of ignorance and continued to reject him.

THE NIGHT JOURNEY

It was during the tenth year of the mission that Muhammad, *ṣalla Allāhu 'alayhi wa sallam,* was to experience the greatest sorrow of his life. His uncle Abu Talib, who had up to then provided him with much needed family protection and support, died. This was followed soon after by the death of his loving wife Khadijah. To add to his grief, the people of Ta'if, to whom he had journeyed to convey the message of Islam, had mercilessly rejected him, sending ruffians to pelt him with stones, making his body stream with blood. It was in this devastating and difficult time that the Prophet, *ṣalla Allāhu 'alayhi wa sallam,* was to be given one of the greatest and most uplifting honours by Allah, glorified and exalted is He. This was the miraculous Night Journey.

On that special night, the angel Gabriel came to Muhammad, *ṣalla Allāhu 'alayhi wa sallam,* and woke him from his sleep. Gabriel then bade him mount what looked like a dazzling white creature named al-Buraq. Soon, with lightning speed, Muhammad was transported to al-Masjid al-Aqsa, the distant place of prayer in Jerusalem.

There on this blessed site, in the heart of Jerusalem, Muhammad, *ṣalla Allāhu ʿalayhi wa sallam*, was met by an assembly of earlier Prophets who gathered behind him as he led them in prayer.

From there Gabriel took him and they ascended through the seven heavens to witness the unseen mysteries of the universe and to see some of the greatest signs of Allah.

According to Tradition, the Prophet said, [22] "When I entered the lowest heaven, I saw a man sitting there with the spirits of men and women passing before him. To one on the right he would smile, saying, "A good spirit from a good body," and of another on the left he would frown and say, "A bad spirit from a bad body." I said, "Who is this, o Gabriel?" He replied, "This is Adam and the persons on the right and left are his offspring. Those on the right are the people of Paradise and those on the left are the people of the Hellfire."

Then Gabriel ascended with Muhammad, *ṣalla Allāhu ʿalayhi wa sallam*, through each subsequent heaven, meeting different Prophets as he went: Jesus, John, Joseph, Aaron, Moses (peace be upon them all), until finally they reached to the seventh heaven. There was a man sitting on a throne at the gate of the Sacred

House. "Never have I seen a man more like myself," said the Prophet, *ṣalla Allāhu 'alayhi wa sallam*. "This was my father Abraham...[23]" Then Gabriel appeared to the Prophet, *ṣalla Allāhu 'alayhi wa sallam*, in all his angelic light and splendour. They had reached the Lote-tree of the utmost boundary, the Sidrat al-Muntaha, veiled by mysterious colours, inexhaustibly indescribable.

MĀ kadhaba al-fu'ādu mā ra'ā • Afa-tumārūnahū 'alā mā yarā •Wa laqad ra'āhu nazlatan ukhrā • 'Inda Sidrati al-muntahā • 'Indahā Jannatu al-ma'wā • Idh yaghsha al-Sidrata mā yaghshā • Mā zāgha al-baṣaru wa mā ṭaghā • Laqad ra'ā min āyāti Rabbihi al-kubrā •

THE HEART FALSIFIED NOT WHAT HE SAW • WILL YOU THEN DISPUTE WITH HIM CONCERNING WHAT HE SEES? • AND VERILY HE SAW HIM YET ANOTHER TIME • BY THE LOTE-TREE OF THE UTMOST BOUNDARY • NEAR IT, THE GARDEN OF ABODE • WHEN THE LOTE-TREE WAS SHROUDED BY WHATEVER ENSHROUDED • THE SIGHT DID NOT SWERVE, NOR DID IT EXCEED • VERILY HE SAW, OF THE SIGNS OF HIS LORD, THE GREATEST.[24]

Migration

MUHAMMAD, *ṣalla Allāhu 'alayhi wa sallam,* had soared to the zenith of Divine heights. It was in this night of supreme spiritual and bodily elevation that he received from Allah Almighty the second noble pillar of Islam: the five daily prayers, and that which was given to no Prophet ever before – the whole world was made as a place of prostration and prayer for Muslims. This was *al-Isra' wa al-Mi'raj,* the Night Journey and Ascension.[25]

On his return, the next morning, after hearing about this miraculous journey, the disbelievers now rejoiced in the opportunity to jeer and mock at Muhammad, *ṣalla Allāhu 'alayhi wa sallam,* even more. They had called him a madman, a soothsayer, a poet and now a liar. Persecution increased and life grew unbearable for the Prophet, *ṣalla Allāhu 'alayhi wa sallam,* and his companions. They were constantly in danger and so they quietly prepared to leave Makkah.

AL-MADINAH

A delegation of those who had embraced Islam from the city of Yathrib, two hundred and fifty miles away, offered their homes and welcomed all Muslims to live in the safety of their city. They especially wanted the Prophet to bring peace to their city torn by tribal feuds and unrest.

The Prophet, *ṣalla Allāhu 'alayhi wa sallam*, accepted. This was to be the *Hijrah*, the Migration. The turning point in Islamic history, from which date the Islamic calendar began: the birth of the first Islamic State; and thus, Yathrib came to be called 'the City of the Prophet' – *Madinat al-Nabi*.

Muhammad, *ṣalla Allāhu 'alayhi wa sallam*, the Messenger of Allah, after 13 years of inviting to Islam and after suffering bitter persecution at the hands of the pagan Arabs, left Makkah together with the small community of Muslims and migrated to where they had been offered peace and security in the city of Madinah. Thus began the second major phase in the mission and life of the Prophet, *ṣalla Allāhu 'alayhi wa sallam*.

THE FIRST CONSTITUTION

In Madinah, the Prophet, *ṣalla Allāhu 'alayhi wa sallam*, became the Head of State. From here, Islam was to blossom. A new brilliant and just social order was born. Its base was the mosque. Here too, Islam's vision for peace amongst all the peoples of the world, of all faiths and races, took shape in what was effectively the first Constitution and Charter of Human Rights and Liberties ever. It guaranteed every citizen freedom, security and justice:

1 Freedom of conscience and worship for Muslim as well as non-Muslim alike.

2 Security and protection from any outside threat or attack.

3 Justice and the prohibition of all crime and immoral practices.[26]

WA al-ladhīna āmanū wa hājarū wa jāhadū fī sabīli Allāhi wa al-ladhīna āwaw wa naṣarū ulā'ika humu al-mu'minūna ḥaqqan, lahum maghfiratun wa rizqun karīm • THOSE WHO BELIEVED AND MIGRATED AND FOUGHT FOR THE CAUSE OF ALLAH AND THOSE WHO TOOK THEM IN AND HELPED THEM — THESE ARE THE BELIEVERS IN TRUTH. FOR THEM IS PARDON AND GENEROUS PROVISION.• [27]

Charity was one of the main features of this new society; greed and selfishness became strangers and were replaced by compassion and concern for all living things. The Prophet, *ṣalla Allāhu 'alayhi wa sallam*, said doing justice between two people is a charity; and assisting a man upon his beast and lifting his baggage is a charity; and answering a questioner with mildness is a charity; and removing that which is an inconvenience to man (such as thorns and stones) is a charity; and a smile to your brother is a charity.[28]

Once a man came up to Muhammad, *ṣalla Allāhu*

'alayhi wa sallam, and begged him for some sheep. There were a large number of them grazing between two hills, so he ordered for them all to be given to him. When the man returned to his village he said, "O people, embrace Islam, for by Allah, Muhammad gives so much, he does not fear poverty."[29]

Here in Madinah, another two more important Pillars of Islam were established. The Muslims were ordered to pay Zakah,[30] the wealth tax due to help the poor and needy, and Fasting in the month of Ramadan[31]. During this period the Prophet, *ṣalla Allāhu 'alayhi wa sallam,* re-married. He was proposed to by many, but apart from 'A'ishah, the daughter of Abu Bakr, his wives were mainly widows of Muslims who had been killed and martyred. However, he always had a special place and memory in his heart for Khadijah, his first wife and beloved partner.[32]

PEOPLE OF THE BOOK

The area of Madinah was also populated by a number of Jewish tribes. The Muslims already felt a close affinity with these 'People of the Book', as the coming of the Prophet had been foretold in the Torah. God had said to Moses:

> 'I will raise them up a Prophet from among their brethren, like unto thee; and I will put My words in his mouth. And he shall speak to them all that I shall command him.'[33]

Who in the Old Testament were the brethren of the sons of Israel if not the sons of Ishmael? Who else could have been the Prophet like unto Moses? Who was more similar to him than the Prophet Muhammad, *ṣalla Allāhu 'alayhi wa sallam?* And according to the sayings of Jesus, the prophecy was also fulfilled:

> 'If I go not away, the Comforter will not come unto you, but if I depart I will send him unto you... He will guide you into all truth; for he shall not speak of himself but whatever he shall hear, that shall he speak...' [34]

Up to this time, Muslims had even prayed in the same direction as the People of the Book, facing the Holy City of Jerusalem.

The believers were now ordered to turn their faces for prayer towards the Holy Mosque in Makkah – the Ka'bah.[35] This historic change in the direction of the prayer symbolized the distinction and honour given to the new Muslim Ummah. As the Muslims were returning to the original faith of Abraham, so in prayer they turned to the first House of Allah erected by him.

PERMISSION TO FIGHT

Apart from the People of the Book, the Makkan chiefs too were displeased.[36] They were still determined to wipe out the new Muslim community and were plotting to attack Madinah. But now, at last, after years of persecution, and torture, permission was given by Allah for Muslims to defend themselves.

UDHINA li-l-ladhīna yuqātalūna bi-annahum ẓulimū wa inna Allāha ʿalā naṣrihim la-Qadīr •

PERMISSION IS GIVEN UNTO THOSE WHO ARE BEING FOUGHT (AGAINST) BECAUSE THEY HAVE BEEN WRONGED; AND INDEED ALLAH IS ABLE TO GIVE THEM VICTORY.• 37

BATTLE OF BADR

The result was the Battle of Badr in the second year after the *Hijrah* in the month of Ramadan. The Makkan army attacked with one thousand men, outnumbering the small Muslim army three to one. But, by the Will of Allah, the outcome was a spectacular victory for the Muslims. Some of the Makkan chiefs who had led the persecutions against the Muslims were killed. Others were taken prisoner and subsequently ransomed. For the first time in history, prisoners of war were fed and sheltered like their captors and treated humanely. This battle was a turning point – the strength and courage of the Believers shocked the Makkans and their allies, but they were still determined to destroy Islam.

In battle after battle, the Muslims proved they could withstand all attacks. After a narrow escape for the believers in the Battle of Uhud the following year,[38] the Quraysh then planned a once and for all assault to destroy the Muslims. They plotted with certain bedouin and Jewish tribes and Hypocrites[39] within Madinah itself.

In the fifth year of *Hijrah*, a force of more than ten thousand marched on Madinah. However, the Muslims were ready: on the advice of Salman the Persian, they had prepared to defend themselves by digging a system of wide trenches around the city.

The Prophet, *ṣalla Allāhu 'alayhi wa sallam*, himself took part in this and while he was digging they sang a refrain:

Allāhumma law lā Anta ma-ihtadaynā
Wa mā taṣaddaqnā wa lā ṣallaynā (yā Rabb)
Allāhumma law lā Anta ma-ihtadaynā
Wa mā taṣaddaqnā wa lā ṣallaynā (yā Rabb)
Fa-anzili al-sakīnata 'alaynā (yā Rabb)
Wa thabbiti al-aqdāma in laqaynā
Allāhumma law lā Anta ma-ihtadaynā...[40]

After a month-long siege, and unable to penetrate the Muslim defences, the pagan army became impatient. Gradually distrust began to spread between the allied forces. Quarrelling amongst themselves and suffering from severe weather conditions, they finally packed up their tents and withdrew.

TREATY OF HUDAYBIYYAH

This was a great victory for Islam. Madinah was never again attacked. In the following year, the 6th after *Hijrah*, a truce was made between the Makkans and the Prophet, *ṣalla Allāhu 'alayhi wa sallam*. Even though the terms were weighed heavily on the side of the Quraysh, this was to be another triumph for Islam and it was called the Treaty of Hudaybiyyah. The period of peace which followed gave many non-Muslims the chance to see for themselves the blessing of the Islamic way of life. As a result, an enormous number of Makkans and tribes embraced Islam.

One day a man from a distant region, with ruffled hair, came to the Messenger of Allah to ask about Islam. The Prophet, *ṣalla Allāhu 'alayhi wa sallam*, said, "You have to offer prayers five times in one day and a night." The man asked, "Is there any more?" The Prophet replied, "No, but if you want to offer extra prayers you can." He continued, "You have to fast during the daylight hours in the month of Ramadan." The man asked, "Is there any more fasting?" He replied, "No, but if you want to offer extra fasts you may." Then the Prophet further said to him, "You have to pay Zakah (obligatory charity)." The man asked, "Is there anything other than Zakah for me to pay?" The Messenger of Allah, *ṣalla Allāhu 'alayhi wa sallam*, said, "No, unless you want to give alms of your own." At that point the man said, "By Allah! I will neither do less nor more than this." The Prophet, *ṣalla Allāhu 'alayhi wa sallam*, remarked, "If he is true to what he says, then he will be successful."[41]

During this period the Prophet, *ṣalla Allāhu 'alayhi*

CALL TO THE RULERS

wa sallam, sent letters to various rulers, including the emperors of the two super-powers of that time, Persia and Byzantium, inviting them to Islam. The Emperor Heraclius was on his way to Jerusalem when he received the letter bearing the Prophet's seal. It read, "From Muhammad the Servant of Allah and His Messenger, to Heraclius, Emperor of Byzantium. Peace be unto him who follows true guidance. I invite you to Islam. Accept it and you will have peace and prosperity and Allah will give you double reward. If you reject, the sins of your subjects will be on you."[42] And the letter ended with a verse of the Qur'an:

QUL yā Ahla al-Kitābi ta'ālaw ilā kalimatin sawā'in baynanā wa baynakum allā na'buda illa Allāha wa lā nushrika bihī shay'an wa lā yattakhidha ba'ḍunā ba'ḍan arbāban min dūni Allāhi, Fa-in tawallaw fa-qūlu ishhadū bi-annā muslimūn •

SAY: O PEOPLE OF THE BOOK! COME TO COMMON TERMS BETWEEN US AND YOU: THAT WE WORSHIP NONE BUT ALLAH, AND THAT WE ASSOCIATE NO PARTNERS WITH HIM, AND THAT WE WILL NOT SET UP FROM AMONGST OURSELVES OTHERS AS LORDS BESIDE ALLAH. THEN IF THEY TURN AWAY, SAY, BEAR WITNESS THAT WE ARE MUSLIMS (SUBMITTING TO HIM). •[43]

Even though the Emperor recognized that this was indeed the Prophet who – according to Scriptures – had been awaited, he felt compelled by loyalty to his chiefs and courtiers to reject the message. And thus, sadly, the winds of fate blew closed the door: the good tidings went unheeded and the Prophet *ṣalla Allāhu 'alayhi wa sallam*'s words inevitably became fulfilled.

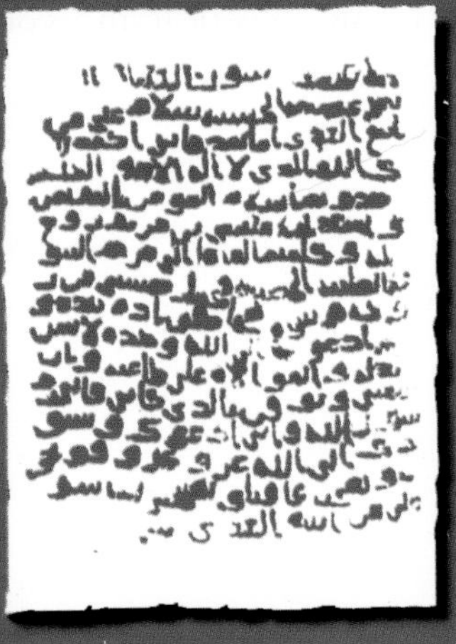

Letter from the Messenger of Allah ﷺ
to the Negus of Abyssinia

Conquest of Makkah

MAKKAH OPENED

MEANWHILE in Arabia, Islam's strength was rapidly growing. Two years after the truce with the Makkans was made, and as its terms were repeatedly violated by the Quraysh, Muhammad, *ṣalla Allāhu 'alayhi wa sallam*, decided to march on Makkah with an army of about ten thousand. What happened was to be an all-time marvel and a landmark in the history of religious conquests. The Prophet, *ṣalla Allāhu 'alayhi wa sallam*, captured the city with hardly a single drop of blood being shed. He rode through the gate mounted on a camel, with his head bowed in humility – as all his trembling enemies looked on.

Yet to their amazement he proceeded to forgive all those who had up to then been bitter enemies of Islam and announced a general amnesty. This was the Day of Victory and the final chapter of the Prophet's life was about to begin.

The conquest of Makkah was over. The enemies of Islam had surrendered and were graciously pardoned. Witnessing the merciful behaviour and character of the Prophet, *ṣalla Allāhu 'alayhi wa sallam,* the people of Makkah voluntarily accepted Islam. The Prophet, *ṣalla Allāhu 'alayhi wa sallam*, entered the Holy Precinct of the sacred Ka'bah. There stood all of the 360 idols and stones, the false gods which the Arabs had bowed to and worshipped for so long. One by one, on the order of the Prophet, *ṣalla Allāhu 'alayhi wa sallam*, the idols were smashed into pieces, thus finally erasing the symbols of idolatry from the Arabian peninsula.

IDOLS SMASHED

At last this House, the sacred Ka'bah, erected by the noble Prophet Abraham and his first son Ishmael, was purified and re-dedicated to the worship of the one and only God, Allah, Lord of all the worlds.

> HUWA al-ladhī arsala Rasūlahū bi-al-hudā wa dīni al-ḥaqqi li-yuẓhirahū 'alā al-dīni kullihī wa law kariha al-mushrikūn •
>
> HE IT IS WHO HAS SENT HIS MESSENGER WITH THE GUIDANCE AND RELIGION OF TRUTH, THAT HE MAY EXALT IT ABOVE ALL RELIGIONS, EVEN THOUGH THE PAGANS MAY DETEST IT.• [44]

It was twenty-one years since the Prophet, *ṣalla Allāhu 'alayhi wa sallam*, had started calling humanity to recognize the One Transcendent God and the Qur'anic revelation had begun. Now Muhammad's mission was coming to a close.

He stayed in Madinah, which effectively became

the capital of the new Muslim world. Delegations from all over Arabia came to embrace Islam at the hands of the Prophet, *ṣalla Allāhu 'alayhi wa sallam*. In addition, he sent groups of believers to various provinces and lands, inviting them to enter Islam. Even with all of Arabia and surrounding lands at his command, he continued to live as a humble servant of Allah. He used to patch his own sandals, sew his clothes and serve his family like any ordinary man.[45]

FAREWELL PILGRIMAGE

It was in the seventh century, ten years after the *Hijrah*, the Prophet was nearing the end of his life on earth. That was the year he performed Hajj, the Pilgrimage, the fifth and final pillar of Islam. Under the scorching sun, on the plains of 'Arafat, Prophet Muhammad, *ṣalla Allāhu 'alayhi wa sallam*, delivered his final sermon:

> "O people! Listen to my words carefully, for I know not whether after this year I shall ever meet you again at this place. O people! Your lives and your property are sacrosanct until you meet your Lord, as are this holy place, this holy day and this holy month. Remember that you will indeed meet your Lord and answer for your deeds. So beware. Whoever of you is holding a trust, let him return it to its rightful owner. All usury is abolished; your capital, however, is yours to keep; wrong not and you shall not be wronged... All bloodshed from the

pagan age of ignorance is to be left unavenged... O people! The Devil has lost all hope of ever being worshipped in this land of yours. Nevertheless, he will try to mislead you in smaller matters. Beware of him, therefore, for the safety of your religion...time has turned and it is as it was the day God created the heavens and the earth. The number of months is twelve; four of them are holy, in which war and fighting are forbidden... You have your rights over your wives and they have rights over you. It is your right that they do not fraternize with anyone of whom you do not approve. But if they do, Allah has permitted you to isolate them within their homes and chastise them without cruelty. But if they abide by your rights, then they have the right to be fed and clothed in kindness. Do treat your women well and be kind to them, for they are your partners and committed helpers... You have taken them only as a trust from Allah and you have their enjoyment only by His permission. So listen to me in earnest, o people! and reason well. I leave behind me two things: the Qur'an and my example (*Sunnah*)[46]. If you follow them you will not go astray. O people! Listen to my words. Know that every Muslim is a brother to every Muslim and that all Muslims constitute one brotherhood. It is only lawful to take from a brother what he gives you willingly, so wrong not yourselves."

The Prophet, *ṣalla Allāhu 'alayhi wa sallam,* then faced the heavens and said: "Be my witness, o Allah, that I have conveyed Your message to Your people." It was then that some of the final words of the Qur'an were revealed:

> AL-yawma akmaltu lakum dīnakum wa atmamtu 'alaykum niᶜmatī wa raḍītu lakumu al-Islāma dīnan •
>
> 'THIS DAY I HAVE PERFECTED YOUR RELIGION FOR YOU, AND HAVE COMPLETED MY FAVOUR UPON YOU, AND HAVE CHOSEN FOR YOU AS YOUR RELIGION AL-ISLAM. • [47]

THE DEATH OF THE PROPHET

A few months after, at the age of 63, Allah Almighty reclaimed his soul. The Prophet Muhammad, *ṣalla Allāhu 'alayhi wa sallam,* passed away in his home in Madinah leaving no more than a few small possessions;[48] with the world at his feet, but not a dinar to his name. Yet the spirit of his message remains as clear and alive today as when it was first delivered – that man may witness the miracle of his life and mission, the beauty and perfection of his call.

LĀ ILĀHĀ ILLA ALLĀH,
MUḤAMMADUN RASŪL U ALLĀH

There is no god but Allah. Muhammad is the Messenger of Allah, *ṣalla Allāhu 'alayhi wa ṣallam.*

Sayings of the Prophet ص

ص This sign represents the salutation *ṣalla Allāhu 'alayhi wa sallam* which is normally pronounced after the name of the Prophet and means: Peace and Blessings of Allah be upon him.

Narrated Abu Hurayrah: Allah's Messenger ص said,"My similitude in comparison with the other Prophets before me is similar to a palace built nicely and beautifully, except for a placement of one brick. The onlookers go about it and wonder at the beauty of its construction except for the place of that brick; so I am that brick, and I am the seal of the Prophets."[49]

Faith

'Faith consists of more than sixty odd branches; and Haya'(modesty) is a branch of faith.'[50]

Knowledge

'Men are mines, like mines of gold and silver, the best of them in the days of ignorance are the best of them in Islam when they have understood (the religion).'[51]

Remembrance

'The example of the one who remembers his Lord (Allah) in comparison with the one who does not remember his Lord is that of the living and the dead.'[52]

Prayer

'If there was a river at the door of anyone of you and he took a bath in it five times a day, would you say there could remain any dirt on him?' They said, 'Not a trace of dirt would be left.' The Prophet ص added, 'That is the example of the five prayers with which Allah annuls evil deeds.'[53]

Earnings

'Nobody has ever eaten a better meal than that which he has earned by working with his own hands.'[54]

Spending

'Allah the Most High said: Spend o son of Adam and (I) shall spend on you.'[55]

Marriage

'When a man marries, he has fulfilled half of the religion; so let him fear Allah regarding the remaining half.'[56]

Conduct

'Certainly the most perfect of believers in faith is one who is best of them in conduct and most affable to his family.'[57]

Parents

'Let his nose be rubbed in the dust, let his nose be rubbed in the dust!' It was said, 'O Messenger of Allah, who is he?' 'He who sees either of his parents during their old age or both of them, but he does not enter Paradise.'[58]

Judging

'A ruler should not judge between two persons while he is angry.'[59]

Visiting the sick

'Verily, Allah, the Exalted and Glorious, will say on the Day of Resurrection: O son of Adam, I was sick but you did not visit Me. He will say: O my Lord, how could I visit Thee when thou art the Lord of the worlds? Thereupon He will say: Didn't you know that a certain servant of Mine was sick but you did not visit him, and were you not aware that if you had visited him, you would have found Me by him.'[60]

Gentleness

'He who is deprived of gentleness is deprived of good.'[61]

Mercy

'Whoever is not merciful to others will not be treated with mercy.'[62]

Anger

'A man petitioned the Prophet ص, 'Advise me!' He said, 'Do not become angry.' The man asked again and again and the Prophet ص said in each case, 'Do not become angry.'[63]

Trust

'Seventy thousand of my Ummah (people) would be admitted into Paradise without rendering any account.' They said, 'Who would they be o Messenger of Allah?' He said, 'Those who do not seek treatment through Ruqya (charms), nor take omens or cauterise, but repose trust in their Lord.'[64]

Qur'an

'The best of you is he who learns the Qur'an and teaches it.'[65]

Destiny

'The Prophet ص drew a square and then drew a line through the middle which extended beyond it; then he drew several small lines attached to that central line and said, 'This is the human being, and this (the square) is his fixed lease of life surrounding him, and this (line) which extends beyond is hope, and these small lines are the troubles which confront him; if one misses him the other will overtake him, and if the other misses him another will overtake him.'[66]

Notes

1. These are the universal words of the Adhan (call) which summon the believers to prayer in mosques around the world. The call echoes up through the heavens, emanating from the tall minarets and awakening mankind to the remembrance and worship of God five times a day.

2. This salutation is regularly pronounced after the name of Prophet Muhammad is mentioned and is usually rendered into English as 'peace be upon him' or 'pbuh'.

3. The building of the Ka'bah, scholars have estimated, must have taken place while Ishmael was a young man (Surah al-Baqarah (2):127). According to Genesis, Abraham was 86 years old when Ishmael was born in the year 1932 BC. Therefore, the date referred to here is about two and a half thousand years prior to the birth of Muhammad, *ṣalla Allāhu 'alayhi wa sallam*, in the year 572 CE – in the third millennium before the *Hijrah*.

4. Qasim, Zaynab, Ruqayyah, Umm Kulthum, Fatimah and 'Abd Allah.

5. Ibn Ishaq, 'The Life of Muhammad', Oxford University Press (1978) p86.

6. Many of the false deities were given female names such as al-Lat, Manat, al-'Uzza. Some were the names of pious people of Noah such as Wadd, Suwa, Yaghuth and Nasr who were deified and idolized many years after their death: Sahih al-Bukhari volume 6 chapter 322 p414-415.

7. This incident can be found mentioned in the collection of Hadith (sayings) of the Prophet, *ṣalla Allāhu 'alayhi wa sallam*, e.g. in Sahih al-Bukhari volume 1. The words *'Mā anā bi-qāri'* can

mean 'What shall I read/recite?' Or alternatively, 'I am not a reader/reciter'.

8. Surah al-'Alaq (96): 1-5.

9. Sahih al-Bukhari, volume 1 chapter 1 p4.

10. Ibid.

11. Surah al-Fatihah (1):1-7.

12. He was given the name Abu Lahab (lit. Father of Flame) after the revelation of Surah al-Lahab (111) following this incident. Sahih al-Bukhari, volume 6, chapter 353 p467 and chapter 227 p276. Cf. Haykal, 'The Life of Muhammad' p85 ATP (1976).

13. Bukhari, volume 8 chapter 31 p29.

14. Surah Sad (38):5.

15. Surah al-Ikhlas (112):1-4.

16. Ibn Ishaq, 'The Life of Muhammad', p119.

17. Sahih Muslim, volume 4 no. 6518.

18. In Abyssinia (Ethiopia today) lived a just and tolerant king who gave sanctuary to the Muslims during the 5th year of Muhammad's mission, *ṣall Allāhu 'alayhi wa sallam*; Ibn Ishaq, 'The Life of Muhammad' p146.

19. Sahih al-Bukhari, volume 3, chapter 5 p373-374.

20. Agreed upon by Bukhari and Muslim (ref. Mishkat al-Masabih [English translation] Book III ch.38 p768).

21. Ahmad, Nasa'i and Bayhaqi, Mishkat al-Masabih, Book I ch.2 p187.

22. Sahih al-Bukhari, volume 1 chapter 1 pp211-214; and volume 5 chapter 41 pp143-148; Sahih Muslim, volume 1 nos. 309 and 322; also Ibn Ishaq, 'The Life of Muhammad.'

23. Sahih Muslim and Ibn Ishaq.

24. Surah al-Najm (53): 11-18.

25. For further Qur'anic reference see Surah al-Isra' (17): 1.

26. Afzalur Rahman, 'Encyclopaedia of Seerah', volume 1 chapter 3 p29: Muslim Schools Trust (1981).

27. Surah al-Anfal (8):74.

28. Agreed by Bukhari and Muslim (ref. al-Nawawi's Forty

Hadith, no.26 and Mishkat al-Masabih, Book 1 ch.3 p300).

29. Sahih Muslim, volume 4 nos. 5728-9.

30. Zakah (lit. purity, increase). This is the Muslim wealth tax: 2.5% of one's yearly surplus savings. On cattle, crops and earth resources the percentage is increased depending on the commodity. Cf. Surah al-Baqarah (2): 177 and Surah al-Tawbah (9):60.

31. Fasting (Siyam) is enjoined on all Believers. Abstinence from food, drink and marital intercourse is obligatory on every adult Muslim, male or female, between dawn and sunset during the 29/30 day month of Ramadan. Exceptions include the sick, menstruating women, mothers after childbirth, the elderly and long-distance travellers. Cf. Surah al- Baqarah (2): 183-187.

32. Before Islam, there was no restriction on the number of wives a man could marry. The Old Testament mentions Prophet Solomon (peace be upon him) as having "seven hundred wives, princesses, and three hundred concubines" (ref. I Kings, 11:3). Prophet David (peace be upon him) is reported to have had 100 wives (ref. Sahih al-Bukhari, volume 7 ch.120 p122). The Qur'an, however, legally limited the number of wives a man could have to four: this was revealed after the Battle of Uhud in 4AH.

The Prophet Muhammad, *ṣalla Allāhu 'alayhi wa sallam*, was the perfect example and model husband. He showed how, according to need and circumstances, a man should behave with one or more wives. It should be remembered that after wars and battles, many men are killed and their families made orphans and widows; therefore, the Prophet's marriages were exemplary in providing security as well as creating love and bondship between families and tribes in the society whose menfolk had been martyred. The Prophet had ten wives after the death of Khadijah. This was a special dispensation by God for Muhammad, *ṣalla Allāhu 'alayhi wa sallam*, alone and no one after him. The names of the wives of the Prophet *ṣalla Allāhu 'alayhi wa sallam* were: Khadijah, Sawda', 'A'ishah, Hafsah, Zaynab (bint Khuzaymah), Umm Salamah, Zaynab (bint Jahsh), Juwayriyyah, Umm Habibah Ramlah,

Safiyyah and Maymunah.

33. Deuteronomy 18:18.

34. John 16:7 and 16:13.

35. Surah al-Baqarah (2):144-150.

36. Until this time, Muslims had faced towards the Distant Mosque (place of prostration) in Jerusalem for prayer. Some of the Jews had used this fact to suggest that Muhammad, *ṣalla Allāhu 'alayhi wa sallam*, had no alternative but to follow their Qiblah (direction). They claimed that this proved their religion to be superior. This command from God to turn in prayer to the original House of worship built by the Patriarch of the Prophets, Abraham, infuriated the Jews. The change also threatened the Makkans who were claiming the right to be custodians of the Ka'bah.

37. Surah al-Hajj (22):39.

38. Uhud is a famous mountain just outside Madinah. This was the site where the Muslims fought their second major battle against the Makkan polytheists.

39. When the Muslim brotherhood was acquiring strength in Madinah, the wicked resorted to duplicity and secret intrigues in which the ringleaders were the disaffected Jews and Hypocrites, those who pretended to be in Islam but who harboured ill will against the Prophet of God, *ṣalla Allāhu 'alayhi wa sallam* (see Surah al-Mujadilah (58):14).

40. Translation:

O Allah! But for You we would not have been guided nor would we have been charitable nor would we have prayed; so send down peace upon us, and make our feet firm if we meet (the enemy)... Sahih al-Bukhari, volume 5 chapter 28 p300.

41. Sahih al-Bukhari, volume 1 chapter35 p39.

42. Sahih al-Bukhari, volume 1 chapter1 p11.

43. Surah Ali 'Imran (3): 64.

44. Surah al-Saf (61):9.

45. Khurram Murad, 'The Life of the Prophet Muhammad', Islamic Foundation, Leicester.

46. This is mentioned in Haykal's Biography as well as Ibn Ishaq's 'Sirat Rasul Allah', although Sahih Muslim's narration only mentions the Book of Allah (volume 2, no.2803).
47. Surah al-Ma'idah(5):3.
48. Bukhari; 'Mishkat al-Masabih', volume 4 ch. 44 no.182.
49. Bukhari; 'Mishkat al-Masabih', volume 4 ch. 44 no.7.
50. Sahih al-Bukhari, volume 1 chapter 3 p18.
51. Muslim; 'Mishkat al-Masabih', volume 1 ch. 4 no.26.
52. Sahih al-Bukhari, volume 8 chapter 68 p278.
53. Sahih al-Bukhari, volume 1 chapter 6 p301.
54. Sahih al-Bukhari, volume 3 chapter 16 p162.
55. Sahih al-Bukhari, volume 6 chapter 155 p168.
56. Bayhaqi, 'Mishkat al-Masabih', volume 2 ch. 27 no.377.
57. Tirmidhi, 'Mishkat al-Masabih', volume 1 ch. 2 no.67.
58. Implying an uncaring individual. Sahih Muslim, volume 4 no.6189.
59. Sahih al-Bukhari, volume 9 chapter 13 p201.
60. Sahih Muslim, volume 4 no.6232.
61. Sahih Muslim, volume 4 no.6271.
62. Sahih al-Bukhari, volume 8 chapter 18 p18.
63. Sahih al-Bukhari, volume 8 chapter 76 p88.
64. Sahih Muslim, volume 1 no.423.
65. Sahih al-Bukhari, volume 6 chapter 21 p501.
66. Sahih al-Bukhari, volume 8 chapter 4 p285.

Editions referred to:
Saḥih al-Bukhari. The translations of the meanings of Saḥih al-Bukhari by Muhammad Muhsin Khan. 4th ed. Beirut, 1405 / 1985.
Mishkat al-Masabih. Al-Hadis. An English translation and commentary of Mishkat-ul-Masabih by Fazlul Karim. Lahore, n.d.
An-Nawawi's Forty Hadith. Translated by Ezzeddin Ibrahim and Denys Johnson Davies. 2nd ed. Damascus, 1977.

Chronology of the Prophet's Life ص

570 CE Muhammad's birth in Makkah; the lonely orphan

576 Mother Aminah dies; grandfather 'Abd al-Muttalib becomes guardian, followed two years later by his uncle, Abu Talib

582 First trading journey to Syria accompanying Abu Talib

595 Marriage to Khadijah. First son Qasim born (599 CE), dies aged 2 years

605 Muhammad helps to rebuild the Ka'bah

610 Angel Gabriel's visitation to Muhammad in Cave Hira – First revelation, *Iqra'*. Khadijah, 'Ali, Abu Bakr and Zayd become Muslims

613 Public preaching of Islam begins

615 First migration (*Hijrah*) of Muslim group to Abyssinia

616 Persecution increases. Muhammad, family and followers are boycotted by Makkans

619 Year of Sorrow: Khadijah and Abu Talib die, Muhammad's preaching in Ta'if rejected

621 Miraculous Night Journey and Ascension through the Seven Heavens

621 Persecution and threats intensify. Preparation for departure to Yathrib

1 AH The Prophet migrates and is welcomed in Madinah
/622 New Constitution declared for the inhabitants of the city

2/623 Change in Qiblah from the Furthest Mosque in Jerusalem to Ka'bah in Makkah. Fasting is enjoined on believers. The Battle of Badr, a great victory for Muslims

4/625 Battle of Uhud, Muslims narrowly defeated

5/627 Battle of Khandaq (the Trench)—the long siege of Madinah by 10,000 unbelievers

6/628 Treaty of Hudaybiyyah, peace terms between the Prophet and the polytheists

7/629 Letters sent by the Prophet to the Khosru and the Emperor of Byzantium and other rulers inviting them to Islam

8/629 Conquest of Makkah by 10,000-strong Muslim army; general amnesty granted and idols smashed

10/632 Last Pilgrimage of the Prophet. Revelation of the Qur'an complete. Death of the Prophet ص

Du'ā'

Rabbanā innanā sami'nā munādiyan yunādī li-al-īmāni an āminū
OUR LORD! WE HAVE HEARD A CALLER CALLING TO FAITH: 'BELIEVE

bi-Rabbikum fa-āmannā, Rabbanā fa-ighfir lanā dhunūbanā wa kaffir
IN YOUR LORD!' SO WE BELIEVED. OUR LORD! THEREFORE FORGIVE US OUR SINS AND REMIT

'annā sayyi'ātinā wa tawaffanā ma'a al-abrār
FROM US OUR EVIL DEEDS AND TAKE OUR SOULS IN DEATH IN THE COMPANY OF THE RIGHTEOUS!

Allāhumma ṣalli 'alā Muḥammadin wa 'alā āli Muḥammadin
O ALLĀH (SHOWER) YOUR BLESSINGS UPON MUHAMMAD AND UPON THE FAMILY OF MUHAMMAD

kamā ṣallayta 'alā Ibrāhīma wa 'alā āli Ibrāhīma
AS YOU HAVE (SHOWERED) YOUR BLESSINGS UPON ABRAHAM AND UPON THE FAMILY OF ABRAHAM

Fī al-'ālamīna innaka Ḥamīdun Majīd
IN ALL THE WORLDS. VERILY, YOU ARE EVER PRAISED, MOST MAJESTIC!

Subḥāna Rabbika Rabbi al-'izzati 'ammā yaṣifūn
GLORY TO YOUR LORD, THE LORD OF HONOUR, ABOVE WHAT THEY ASCRIBE

wa salāmun 'ala al-Mursalīn wa al-Ḥamdu lillāhi Rabbi al-'ālamīn
AND PEACE (BE) UPON THE MESSENGERS AND ALL PRAISE (BE) TO ALLAH, LORD OF THE WORLDS.